Front Cover: *Christ in Majesty* on the West
Front of Wells Cathedral, photograph © the
author.

Forward

This short reflection is a response to questions of faith and doubt that have arisen following the placing of a temporary sculpture on the West Front of Wells Cathedral. This reflection is a personal response rather than a corporate one. Although I am a canon at the Cathedral, it is from me, rather than from the Cathedral as a whole. It is also only a partial response inasmuch as the sculpture and the whole of the West Front are there for each of us to make our own responses. This reflection is therefore not supposed to be the final word on the sculpture, on the Cathedral or on any other matter. It is offered in the hope that it may be of some use to others in forming their own ideas.

Rob James

The Feast Day of St. Giles, 2021.

A context and introduction

Wells Cathedral is many things to many people. For some, it is a place of deeply personal prayer and reflection. For others, it is a place of wonderful liturgy and music. Some see it as a glorious example of early English architecture, with the West Front as one of the best surviving examples of grand thirteenth century sculptural design. Still others will see it as a venue for live music and cultural events. It is easy to claim that the building was created with one purpose in mind: as a place for the expression of communal faith. But of course, those who ordered its creation had many motives. Faith was certainly one motive, but other questions about power are not far from the surface either. Human motives are rarely completely pure. But be this as it may, whatever else it may be, Wells Cathedral is indeed a great monument to faith.

Given this, it may be surprising and even, for some, upsetting, to find that from August 2021, for eighteen months, there is a sculpture on the West Front going by the name of 'DOUBT.'

It occupies an empty niche where once another figure, now lost, would have stood. DOUBT is by the internationally renowned sculptor Sir. Antony Gormley. It is of an 'orthogonal' nature – simply meaning that it is not a fully-formed figure, but is instead made up of cuboid blocks. It is humanoid in form, but it is not fully like a human in appearance. This is in sharp contrast to other figures on the West Front. Most are of humans and look like humans. Of greatest prominence is Christ himself, risen and in majesty, right at the top of the West Front. The figures were intended to be fully formed, with facial features, hands, feet, and so on. Some of the original sculptures retain many of their features, but most are seriously weathered, such that they have become far more abstract than originally intended. It is therefore not quite true to suggest that an abstract piece has been placed into a collection of sculpture that is not abstract, for much of it is abstract, at least now, even if not originally. Also in terms of form, the other sculptures on the West Front stand firmly in their niches, looking directly out to the West. In contrast, DOUBT stands on the edge of the niche, looking to one side. Read in this context, the whole sculpture radiates doubt, both in terms of what it looks like and of its positioning. Some will love the form of the sculpture temporarily on the West Front and some will loathe it. That is the nature of art. But whether one likes or loathes, or even is simply left cold by it is not especially relevant or interesting. If everyone had to like the form of a sculpture before it was installed, then no public art would ever happen. Of rather more interest is whether a figure of doubt, in any form, has any place on the West Front.

In answer to this question, it rather depends on how the relationship between faith and doubt is viewed. On one assessment, they are opposites and are in opposition to one another. In this way of thinking, 'doubt' is the absence of 'faith,' and may even be something that is actively opposed to faith. But there are other ways of thinking about these two categories which suggest that doubt is an aspect of faith or a stage in the development and deepening of faith rather than something that exists in opposition to faith. It is this more positive understanding of doubt that is explored here.

What follows is a short reflection on the theme of faith and doubt. The reflection begins with a consideration of doubt as a psychological aspect of faith – the 'shadow' of faith that is a psychological inevitability of having faith. Here it will be suggested that doubt is inevitable and that the way of dealing with it productively is to own it and integrate it into faith rather than to deny it. Next, there follow some thoughts about the importance of being honest about doubt if faith is to be discovered. In particular, this section will discuss St. Thomas and will also make use of a poem by Tennyson. Just like the importance of the acknowledgement of doubt from a psychological-shadow point of view, it is also true that it is important to be honest about doubt if a real depth of faith is to be discovered. Next, there follow some thoughts about the way in which faith can suddenly seem to be real and tangible, only to disappear before it can be grasped. Here it will be suggested that such moments of faith become love for the one experiencing them and that this love can shape life. The incarnation is briefly discussed at the end of the reflection, in particular to consider how difficult it is to accept this teaching without first doubting. In concluding, it will be suggested that love has the final word. We humans can discover that we are loved, and this realisation is arrived at through an honest faith that integrates doubt.

The shadow of faith

Humans are complex beings and this is why they provide endless opportunities for study and, maybe more importantly, for understanding. Whether or not you go all the way with Carl Jung's psychological framework, what Jung has to say about personality and its shadow is of particular use in thinking about faith and doubt. In very brief summary, Jung discovered the pragmatic truth that all humans have elements of their personalities that they suppress because of the socio-cultural environment in which they find themselves. Jung called these hidden, suppressed parts of ourselves 'shadows.' In essence, any culture will inevitably create shadows. 'Culture' might be how entire nations live, but could equally be the 'culture' of a particular family or of an organisation. The 'shadows' are not inherently 'bad' or 'evil' but are simply poor fits for the culture in which the individual who has these particular shadows exists. But the shadows are true parts of personality and can emerge, often unhelpfully and unexpectedly. Someone can suddenly become apoplectically angry over an apparently minor issue, maybe even surprising the person who is angry. The anger appears to have come from nowhere, but, Jung would suggest, the anger is caused by something that has touched a suppressed part of the personality. However, this is not all bad news. If people can work out what their shadows are, then they can come into a deep awareness of integral but previously unknown parts of their personality. Ultimately, Jung suggests that if shadows can be embraced, then this can lead to great creativity and a deep, lived experience of a happy, integrated life.

Shadows are not only the property of individuals. They are also inescapable within organisations. All organisations have their own particular culture. Whether it is the police, a political party, the Mothers' Union, the Women's Institute, a bank, a bakery or a cathedral, a diocese or the Church in general, all have their own particular cultures. Because they have culture, there will also be shadow, things that the organisation suppresses, does not talk about, because to do so would break some sort of perceived but unspecified code. Such organisational shadows can break out in unhelpful ways no less than in the case of individuals. It is easy to find examples of this from the world of banking, such as when the LIBOR rate was rigged. The details of the crime are as simple as they are boring, simply consisting of boosting profit by illegally overriding market forces by slightly altering the rate at which banks could borrow from one another. The shadow within the banks where individuals were found to be doing this may well have been the acceptance that profit was king. The banks were well run, had ethical as well as legal controls in place and so on. But the shadow of greed for profit broke through and the controls were suddenly found to be inadequate. Since then, effort has been made to understand the shadow, which is the only way in which it can be both prevented from breaking through, but also be better utilised to drive the turning in of a healthy, but also legal, profit.

In the case of the Church, certainly for both the Church of England and the Roman Catholic Church but also for a good many other parts of the Church, the organisational shadow that has been most in evidence of late has been the need to protect the Church's reputation. Stories of abusers being moved on rather than confronted, of abusers being protected and victims being hung out to dry abound. There was an assumption that the reputation of the Church came first, and tragically this became an idol to which many were sacrificed. Recently, various churches in Canada have been reeling from the tragic case of the residential schools scandal, where, at least historically, reputation was put far above the welfare of indigenous children and communities. Whether any church has yet entirely got to grips with the organisational shadows that let abuse go unchecked remains to be seen, although great strides have been made.

In the context of organisations, culture is often expressed as 'brand.' The shadows are all those things that are 'off brand' but which are nevertheless the lived experience of the organisation. But they are suppressed because everyone wants to be seen as 'on brand' and 'on message.' Attempts to keep organisational shadows suppressed do not work for ever. The respectability of the Church has been damaged for ever by scandals driven by the desire for respectability. It is a bit of a cliché, but it also happens to be true that 'it is the cover up that kills you.' If the Church had only been open from the start about the situation with abusers, then not only would many never have become victims, but also the Church's reputation would be far better than it is today. The 'brand' of respectability may well be a good thing, at least it is not a bad thing in and of itself, but the shadow is 'respectability at any cost,' which ends up costing everything when it blows up.

Since the temporary sculptural addition to the West Front was proposed, and also since its installation, a number of people have written to me or spoken to me to voice their opposition to it. Some have worried about the form, but far more have been concerned about its name. From the perspective of Jung's ideas of psychological shadow, this suggests that there may be a widespread fear of doubt or inability to deal productively with doubt on the part of Christians. And yet it seems inevitable that this means that there are vast wells and aquifers of doubt that run below the surface of faith for many. Such doubt, unacknowledged and repressed, can be dangerous to faith. It can punch its way through to the surface in such a fountain that all is covered by it in an uncontrolled explosion. But, if such doubt is acknowledged and worked with it can be the very place where great creative insight can be found. To think of the church in organisational terms, the 'brand' that is being worked with here is 'faith' or 'faithfulness.' One correspondent acknowledged that doubt is a feature of 'many people's minds, but for Christians? Surely not.' Such an absolute position that a particular experience or thought (in this case, doubt) cannot be a part of lived reality is a classic *leitmotif* of the suppression of some element of reality. In this case, it was clearly inconceivable to my correspondent that doubt could be any part of the lived reality of faith. It is something that is conceptualised, probably subconsciously, as so dangerous and explosive that it cannot be allowed any hearing, any acknowledgement whatsoever. The message is this: Christians do not doubt. Faith is absolute and unquestioned. Maybe, even, you cannot be a real Christian if you have doubts.

The world, human experience and faith are not this simple. The reality is that doubts abound. Simply to suppress and deny them does not take them away, nor does it do anything to 'solve' them. Indeed, it may be that not all doubts are solvable, but that the faithful Christian has to learn to live a life of faith with their doubts as part of the package. To deny that doubts exist is to run the danger of asserting that everything either read in the Bible or taught by the Church has to be accepted as fact. Having no doubts about any of this at all would mean that it is impossible to accept modern Physics or Biology (for the world was made about 6000 years ago, created pretty much as we see it today). The assertion that Christians do not doubt is in danger of making faith into nothing more than a fairy story that simply cannot be accepted as true or real by anyone. But more than this, it also runs the risk of missing the point of faith altogether, which we will return to below. But to come back to the idea of doubt as faith's shadow, the idea of denying modern science is a case in point. If the person of faith has to deny modern science, then they are forced to suppress any glimmer of possibility that science could be right about, say, evolution. Over time, it is easy to see how the pressure of this builds up. Eventually, such pressure cannot be contained. The reality explodes to the surface: it is realised that science is correct about evolution and, simultaneously, that the Bible is not scientifically correct, which had been a suppressed doubt. In this wild explosion of realisation, it is likely that all faith is swept away. If, alternatively, such doubt had been brought into the open, discussed with others and integrated into the life of faith, then there is nothing to do with doubt left to explode as it has already been acknowledged and integrated, probably leading to a far deeper and more creative faith than had such doubt been suppressed.

The exception to what has been said above is the case of the sect or cult that demands very precise adherence to their own doctrine. People are sucked into such doubt-free zones for various reasons and once such a group has control of a person's life (which, in extreme cases, can be total), it can be very difficult to leave. Some courageous people manage it when their doubts or negative experiences become too much. But many remain in such organisations because they have become their entire world. Looking from the outside, it is a fantasy world. But from the inside, it makes great sense. If only mixing with those who agree with you entirely, all agreeing with the defined doctrine of a group, then it becomes possible to just about suppress doubt. For everyone else, such suppression should provide a valuable lesson.

Even within mainstream Christianity, there is a question about exactly which version of Christianity a faithful person espouses. Variations in doctrine exist between different Christianities. It may well be that the faithful and orthodox Roman Catholic is very happy to accept the Doctrine of Papal Infallibility. Very little is actually covered by this doctrine; it has been rarely invoked. But even the concept is likely to be doubted by some Roman Catholics and certainly by most non-Roman Catholic Christians. So doubt must be allowed for individual beliefs within a faith. As mentioned above, within particular sects there are tight rules about what followers must acknowledge, and it can take great courage to break out of such organisations when doubt about too many specifics becomes too great to remain. But in general, doubt about certain beliefs must be acknowledged as a standard part of the experience of the faithful. Is it possible to have doubts and still to remain faithful? The answer has to be 'yes' unless refuge is to be sought from doubts in sects and cults and/or the risk is run of abandoning faith altogether when doubts surface in an uncontrolled way.

Psychologically speaking, doubt is a shadow that is a part of faith. It is created as an inevitable consequence of having faith. But doubt is not to be feared. Doubt is only problematic for faith when it is unprocessed and suppressed. Doubt that is integrated into the life of faith leads to a deeper faith, and a faith that is not blown around by what one finds in the world, nor, indeed, blown apart altogether when doubts arise. A faith that integrates doubt is a faith fit for the real world. It is not a fairy tale, but a lived reality.

It is not make-believe but instead provides creative space for reflecting upon the world in all of its complexity. A faith that integrates doubt is a faith that one can live by and through, day to day. Seen in these terms, doubt is unavoidable and the choice is whether to integrate it and have a well-rounded faith or to suppress and deny it, instead possessing a fragile, thin faith. The integration of doubt is foundational to healthy faith and this will now be explored in more detail by thinking about some famous Christians who have doubted, in particular St. Thomas.

St. (doubting) Thomas and honest doubt

St. Thomas is one of the better-known disciples of Jesus. He is often known as 'doubting Thomas' because the episode he is most famous for in the New Testament is about his doubts in the Resurrection of Jesus. The story is recounted in John 20.24-29. In the first part, Jesus appears to his close disciples in the room where they are meeting. However, Thomas was not with everyone else and so misses out on seeing Jesus. That Jesus should appear like this is an astonishing thing because he has just been killed and buried. Even though all of his close friends tell him that this has occurred, Thomas just cannot believe it. Then, a week later, the events unfold much as before, except that this time Thomas is in the room when Jesus arrives. This enables Jesus to comment on how happy those are who have believed without having to see him physically.

A few years ago, Thomas featured on the comedy sketch show on BBC Radio 4, the *John Fennimore Souvenir Programme*. In the sketch,

Thomas was complaining that he was usually known as Thomas the Doubter. He thought that this was rather unfair as he was the only disciple (other than Judas) to carry a negative connotation in his name. Why, he asks, is Peter not known as Peter the Denier. It is so unfair! But of course, he's not really any worse than any of the other disciples, although his story is memorable for its visual and visceral qualities, with Jesus inviting Thomas to touch the wounds still borne in his risen body. The cry of unfairness put into Thomas' mouth by Fennimore has quite a lot of justification. Peter is famous for denying Christ prior to his death and although he is remembered for this, he is mostly remembered for other things.

In fact, doubt is one of the things that Peter is remembered for. In Matthew 14, Jesus walks on the water and Peter walks out to him, having to be rescued by Jesus when he takes his eyes off him, becomes frightened by the storm and begins to sink. Jesus then asks Peter why he doubted, implying that he needed to have more faith. Doubt is at the core of Peter's experience in this story, for he doubts and almost drowns. In fact, doubt seems to be built into faith as the disciples experienced it. Right at the end of the Gospel according to Matthew, even though the risen Jesus was standing right in front of his disciples, an enigmatic phrase is to be found: 'but some doubted' (Matthew 24.17). These are the same disciples who went on to spread the message of Jesus' resurrection. This is even more remarkable than the story of Thomas doubting Jesus' resurrection, as these are (unspecified) individuals who have just seen something with their own eyes. But Thomas is the one who is saddled with the title of doubt.

Maybe this is in part because what Thomas did next is not recorded in the Bible. This means that his story has faded out of knowledge and the last thing that most people remember him for is doubting and (if they have read the whole passage) also for coming to believe. But we do know, at least in an approximate fashion, what he did. He travelled to more unknown places than any of Jesus' other early followers, far beyond the bounds of the Roman Empire into Persia and India. The Christians of South India are known as the St. Thomas Christians and they trace their faith back to his arrival in their country. Academics argue about where Thomas actually went in India, but that he travelled far beyond the bounds of the Roman world seems to be historically correct. Precisely where he went is not really the point, the point is that Thomas – doubting Thomas – spread the message of Jesus Christ far and wide. Over the centuries, numerically his mission met with less success than the Christians who remained within the Roman Empire. But this has to do with the politicians of the Empire getting behind the faith and has more to do with later generations than it does to do with Peter or Paul. So it is reasonable to suggest that Thomas was at least as courageous and faithful as any of the other early missionary disciples, and arguably more so. He went where very few had gone before, he had to learn languages he'd never even heard of, he had to travel thousands of miles over very inhospitable terrain and he had to speak to people who had no background in monotheism at all, no knowledge of Judaism; he had none of the familiar pegs on which to hang his message. And yet, he persevered.

Something to note for both Thomas and Peter and the unnamed disciples from Matthew in the stories recounted above is that doubt was not the end of the road of faith, but instead was part of the road. The stories about Peter and Thomas, as they are told in the gospels, suggest that their doubt played an important role in their development. Imagine a different scenario, one in which Thomas had falsely claimed to accept his friends' account of meeting the risen Christ. Maybe, before the week was even out, he would have realised that he could not keep up this charade and quietly slipped away from Jerusalem to resume his old life. He would have missed the second encounter with Jesus. Or with Peter, maybe he could have suppressed all doubts and kept on walking on the water. But would he then have been able to keep his doubt suppressed forever? It seems unlikely. In their two quite different stories, both men learnt to be open about their doubt, learning too that this very human experience did not disqualify them from the love of God or from doing God's work. Indeed, their doubt is a place from which to reach out towards God.

But doubt expressed is not only about the one expressing it. Particularly in the case of Thomas, how his friends reacted to his experience was very important. In the story, they do not cast him from the group because he does not believe as they do. Instead, he is kept close to the group, so much so that he is with them when Jesus returns. There is a lesson here for the Church about how doubt can be handled productively. There is no point in trying to pretend it doesn't exist. Allowing people to 'belong' in a full and meaningful way is more important than trying to insist that they are entirely signed up to all of Church doctrine, or even to what most would describe as the core of doctrine. Expressing unsuppressed doubt shows engagement with such beliefs far more than simple but mindless acceptance shows. If the community can allow these experiences and not try to foreclose them through urgent remedial 'teaching,' then the person going through such experiences can have the space to work them out and to reach beyond them.

There is a sense in which for Thomas, and for others besides, that as doubt is named so is faith begun. There is a famous poem by Alfred Lord Tennyson that expresses this with exquisite elegance. It was penned in memory of his friend Arthur Henry Hallam, who was also Tennyson's sister's fiancé. It was written over a three-year period after Hallam died suddenly of a stroke at the age of just twenty-two. It therefore expresses various different moments of grief that Tennyson was feeling, including a certain amount of anger at what had happened, and also doubt. There is one particularly famous line and the reader may spot it as they read through the poem, but it is good to have that line in its proper context.

You say, but with no touch of scorn,
    Sweet-hearted, you, whose light-
  blue eyes
    Are tender over drowning flies,
You tell me, doubt is Devil-born.

I know not: one indeed I knew
    In many a subtle question versed,
    Who touch'd a jarring lyre at first,
But ever strove to make it true:

Perplext in faith, but pure in deeds,
    At last he beat his music out.
    There lives more faith in honest
  doubt,
Believe me, than in half the creeds.

He fought his doubts and gather'd
  strength,
    He would not make his judgment
  blind,
    He faced the spectres of the mind

And laid them: thus he came at length

To find a stronger faith his own;
 And Power was with him in the
night,
 Which makes the darkness and the
light,
And dwells not in the light alone,

But in the darkness and the cloud,
 As over Sinai's peaks of old,
 While Israel made their gods of gold,
Altho' the trumpet blew so loud.

The famous line is 'There lives more faith in honest doubt, Believe me, than in half the creeds.' But the context that goes around this is important and bolsters what the poem is claiming in this line. To begin with, Tennyson, speaking maybe for himself, maybe for his friend, but also for anyone who has been public about doubt, notes that there are those who say that doubt is of the Devil. Some see it as essentially evil. But Tennyson knows that this is just not the case and that the honesty of expressed doubt is itself a form of faith. Indeed, it is a more honest faith than a creed that is said but not believed. Tennyson then speaks of 'fighting' with doubt. We might more usually use the term 'wrestling' with doubt. In other words, the poem encourages those who doubt not to pretend that doubt does not exist, but rather to engage with it, to keep working away at it. Then, Tennyson speaks of the discovery of a 'stronger faith' through this process of doubt and of working with it. The final stanza is especially interesting. Here Tennyson references the moment in Exodus 32 when Israel chose to worship other gods, mere images, rather than God. Taken with the previous stanza, it may suggest that Tennyson is noting that God was actually present in the darkness of the cloud on the mountain, rather than in the sun-lit valley where the images were being made. Sometimes, the poetry is suggesting, God is found where it is hard to see the way, where darkness has descended. God is not always present in a way that God can be easily and simply grasped. To claim such a thing, to deny the darkness of doubt, is to end up worshipping not the real God, but the gaudy image of an imagined-god.

Both Thomas and Tennyson discovered something important about the relationship between doubt and faith. If properly handled, it is not that one displaces the other. Through the expression of doubt, and through being allowed (or even encouraged) to express that doubt by the community in which one finds belonging, then it is possible to own, accept, process and integrate that doubt into life. This leads to a faith which is real rather than a fantasy that is easily torn down by the vicissitudes of life. God is present in the apparent darkness of doubt. With the author of Psalm 139, it might be observed that, for God, 'light and darkness are both alike.' God can operate in and through human doubt, and humanity can see this, so long as the honesty expressed by Thomas and analysed and articulated by Tennyson is present. Such honest doubt is the beginning or deepening of faith.

The flickerings of faith and love

High up on the West Front of Wells Cathedral, right in the middle, is a sculpture of the risen Christ. As a whole the West Front is a picture of the final judgement and maybe too of Heaven. Below Christ there are the Apostles and then the Angels. Below the Angels, wrapping right around the West Front there is a series of sculptures of people being raised from their graves. The figure of Christ, risen and in majesty, presides over this scene. This is the sculpture on the front cover of this reflection. The photograph used for the front cover was taken in the evening, just before the Sun went down. At that time of day, the West Front changes colour, glowing red and gold in the last light of the day. The light also picks out a lot of detail of the sculptures, which come alive in this light as at no other time in the day. Sometimes at night the Cathedral is floodlit, but even with this level of artificial light, the figures are more stone than living presence. There is something about the light of the setting Sun that is transformative. It is a dramatic sight, and there is no more dramatic part of it than the figure of Christ. The picture on the cover of this reflection cannot quite capture the vitality of it, and it needs to be seen in the flesh, so to speak.

The transformation of the West Front only lasts for a short while, fifteen minutes or so at the end of the day, so long as there is not too much cloud. It is a fleeting, temporary sight. Personally, I find the memory of it persists and draws me back to the West Front as often as possible at this moment. In times past and on days when the floodlights are not on, this greatest moment to see the West Front then rapidly fades and it can hardly be seen at all, for it is dark. This is so often how faith is. There are moments when we catch a glimpse of the transcendent, of that which moves us beyond ourselves. There may even be moments of clarity. But most people find that these are moments and that faith is often about living between these moments, in a lack of clarity and even in darkness. Faithful living is often about living in the hope that another such moment of contact with the transcendent will come. They will not be as regular as the turning of the Earth leading to the Sun sinking into the Western horizon once a day. Indeed, it is their unpredictability that necessitates living in faith. For the most faithful, one such moment is all that is required.

St. Paul experienced something significant when he was still called Saul and was travelling to Damascus to persecute the Christians there. Two slightly different accounts of this are given in Acts 9.1-22 and Galatians 1.11-17. But the essence is that Saul experienced something he knew to be, in what might called a moment of clarity, the presence of the risen Jesus. The fuller version of this occurrence is given in Acts, which has Saul immediately becoming blind and then going to Damascus where he was prayed for by a Christian called Ananias. Saul then regained his sight and was baptised. As Acts presents this, Saul had a moment of clarity, but did not really understand what it was all about. He was then in literal darkness – surely a metaphor for his inner darkness. He then, literally, sees the light and is baptised into the infant Church. Paul presents himself as always very sure. Indeed, he was sure he was right when persecuting the church and he was sure he was right when, re-named Paul, he was preaching his message of the Lordship of Jesus. But at least as Acts tells the story, there is darkness that follows the initial clarity.

In a similar manner, at the end of Luke (24.13-35), there is the very familiar story of the Road to Emmaus. This story is set on the day of the resurrection of Jesus, a Sunday. In this story, two disciples walk away from Jerusalem to a village called Emmaus. They are talking about Jesus, about his death and about what they have heard – a rumour that his tomb was empty and that he had been raised from the dead. They are obviously doubtful of the truth of this story and are a picture of dejection. They are met by someone on the road whom they take to be a stranger, but who is actually Jesus. He walks with them and explains to them that the Messiah had to die and that it was natural that he would then 'enter into his glory.' Something stirs within them and when they reach Emmaus, they invite the stranger in to continue the conversation. At supper, the stranger breaks the bread and in that instant they recognise that he is Jesus. Immediately, Jesus vanishes. The disciples rush back to Jerusalem to tell the other followers of Jesus, to find that the risen Jesus has also appeared to Simon Peter.

It is significant that doubt is not hidden away in the story of the Emmaus Road. It is foundational to the arrival at the belief that Jesus had indeed risen from the dead. The wrestling with the story that the two disciples on the road had heard, that Jesus had risen, is important for their eventual acceptance of the truth they then perceived. Rather like Saul/Paul these two had a moment of clarity in which they saw the truth of the resurrection. But it was only after much discussion, much going over things in their minds, with one another and with an-other too. Then, once they had seen what they then realised to be the truth, Jesus vanished. This is such a compelling story because this is how faith is for most people. Just as something is perceived, it vanishes, or becomes just out of reach. In another resurrection story (John 20.11-18) Jesus meets Mary Magdelene and once she has realised who he is and the implication of this (that he had risen from the dead), Jesus says something that seems strange. He says "Do not hold on to me, for I have not yet ascended to the Father. Go instead to my brothers and tell them, 'I am ascending to my Father and your Father, to my God and your God.' But maybe he tells her not to hold on to him precisely because it is not possible to hold on to something or someone who is embodying transcendence. It is not possible to grasp in one's hand, so to speak, the moments of faith that can form a life of faithful living even in the darkness.

To return briefly to Thomas, whose encounter with Jesus was mentioned above, it is noticeable that Jesus essentially says the opposite to him from his instruction to Mary. Jesus invited Thomas to touch him. But the story contains no mention of such a physical contact actually being made. As soon as the offer is made, Thomas falls to his knees and acknowledges Jesus. Faith is not to be grasped. Faith flickers into being, appears tangible, but cannot be grasped and it is the engagement with the world in the light of such moments held in the memory that constitute the faithful life, lived in the absence of the momentary experience.

As the sculpture of the risen Jesus in majesty on the West Front of Wells Cathedral is most perfectly illuminated only by the dying of the light, making it a fleeting experience, so too with faith. Saul thought that Jesus rising from the dead was a dangerous heresy, the disciples on the road to Emmaus did not believe that Jesus had risen and nor did Mary Magdelene or Thomas. Paul experiences Jesus and is plunged into the dark. Jesus breaks the bread and vanishes. Mary is instructed not to hold on to him; Thomas does not touch him. And yet, this disparate group of people all had a profound experience that shaped their lives, despite not being able to take hold of it, examine it and keep it with them always. It was not theirs to keep hold of. Rather these moments are moments of light in the darkness, moments in which that which is transcendent was glimpsed, moments in which the deep truth of reality was observed, despite the doubts and, at least for some of those noted here, in part because of the doubts.

This is not unfamiliar to the faithful in today's world. It may be that there is much to doubt and that after wrestling with these doubts, faith will either suddenly or gradually emerge. The stories in the Bible tend to be of sudden revelation or experience. But most find it a far more gradual process. Nevertheless, there will still be moments when things suddenly seem to fall into place, only to vanish just as rapidly. This is not an intellectual process. It is quite possible to know all the doctrine, all the 'theory,' and even to intellectually ascent to it without it touching one's inner being. Another way of putting this is to say it is possible to know intellectually without ever loving what one knows. Faith is, among other things, about falling in love.

To illustrate this, the English word 'belief' is of great help. It is based on the older word 'lief' meaning a thing that is beloved. To think of beliefs as things that are truly loved elevates them beyond mere 'things' or items of mental furniture. Something that is believed in this sense is no mere opinion. It shapes the life of the one who loves it. It is of deep and abiding power. There is no need to have all aspects of faith and belief pinned down and fully explained, because love is always beyond final explanation. Beliefs are instead mysteries to be drawn ever deeper into. There is always more and a final explanation or complete analysis is impossible. Such beliefs, such loves, taken together, give rise to the overall faith, which might therefore be described as a love of the mysteries that are beloved.

St. Claire of Assisi tells us that that which is loved is important for human identity. She tells us that both what and who we love shape what we become. In such a context of love, doubt can play a part. Indeed, doubt must play a part. If doubt is the psychological shadow, then in creating a 'culture' of faith, of beloved mysteries, it is inevitable that any or all aspects of this could be doubted and probably will be doubted. If we are to leave the frothy surface of faith and dive in deep, then acknowledging doubt is inescapable. With the help of doubt, along with St. Thomas, Tennyson, the disciples on the road to Emmaus and with others besides, we can be honest about our doubt, thus holding open the door to a deeper experience of faith. As we gradually experience moments of light and clarity, and love that which we cannot quite grasp, we are constantly called deeper into the life of faith and even in the very deepest mire of doubt we are called beyond our doubt. It can take great courage to step beyond it, and that courage will only come by acknowledging it and owning it. That which we love calls us to step out and to discover more. We may even discover that that which we love, loves us too, and even before we loved. But none of that is possible without the honesty, searching and work that doubt calls us to. As we love and find that we are loved, then we are gradually shaped by that love.

A Word to conclude

The Gospel of John begins 'in the beginning was the Word, and the Word was with God, and the Word was God.' This divine Word is that person of God incarnated in Jesus Christ. The Greek for 'Word,' *logos*, can mean just a word or can also mean logic and reason. But the way it is expressed in John defies all final analysis. John is saying what Christian tradition has come to accept as orthodoxy – that God, in all of God's divine and infinite power and authority became incarnate as a human being, limited and finite. Anyone who simply accepts this has either been given a very particular grace by God, or they have not really thought about it. *Logos* may imply 'reason' or 'logic' but the incarnation defies all logic. Logically, infinity cannot be contained in the finite. The Divine Creator cannot be contained in creation. And yet, that is the implication of the incarnation. Despite appearances, God has done something new and otherwise impossible. It is quite natural to doubt the incarnation. Indeed, it would be surprising to find someone who has come across the idea of the incarnation, and who subsequently takes it seriously, not to have processed doubts about it. To take it seriously, to live in the light of the incarnation, to love this belief, presupposes some level of struggle and doubt. Not to have engaged with, or to continue to be engaged with, this struggle and doubt is to imply a form of Christian faith that lives at the surface. If anyone else questions the incarnation or points out the logical problems, such a one is in real danger of abandoning the faith altogether or retreating into the kind of denial that simply keeps them from going deeper. The shadow of doubt is the place where the doctrine of the incarnation, and any doctrine, can be engaged with rather than just accepted or denied. Even as beliefs are loved they can (and maybe should) be doubted so that their depths can be revealed.

Throughout the Gospel of John and throughout the three associated letters, also in the New Testament, Jesus is presented as the incarnation of ultimate love. A verse often used at weddings is from the first letter of John, 1 John 3.16, 'God is love, and those who live in love abide in God, and God lives in them.' As mere human beings engage with the things of God, even in their finitude and smallness, the infinite depths of God can be opened. Faith into which doubt has been well integrated is the best place to be drawn ever deeper into God's very being of love, as we love the things of God, live the life of faith and discover that we are loved.

Doubt is an inevitability and not something to become concerned with or obsessed by. It is inevitable because it is the shadow of faith and so will exist alongside faith. Doubt is inescapable, but it is not to be feared. It is a sign of thoughtful engagement with faith, and is a strength rather than a weakness. It is possible to push it down or away, but ultimately this is not productive or sustainable. If there is a desire to get beyond a surface level, frothy faith, it is important to lay aside false certainty and to engage with the deeper reality of faith and doubt. This is the honest approach taken by St.

Thomas, Tennyson and others. It did not end in them abandoning faith, but in deepening it. Such honesty can lead to moments of faith, light and clarity, arrived at suddenly or gradually. Having the courage to live in the midst of doubt is vital and hones the ability to see beyond and outside of doubt, even as it is experienced. Moments of faith, light and clarity are real but the intensity of them does not last, even if the memory does, and doubt does not disappear. But the life of faith is lived beyond such moments, integrating them into the daily doubts and giving direction to life. Even in the darkness, we can learn to love the transcendent we are drawn towards, and we can allow ourselves to be shaped by that love.

As we live faithfully alongside doubt, the deep and transcendent reality of the creation and the Creator can be revealed to us. And the final word is love.

For further exploration

If you would like to explore the ideas of faith and doubt further, then the following may be of use to you:

Brian McLaren, *Faith After Doubt: Why Your Beliefs Stopped Working and What to Do About It*, (London: Hodder and Stoughton, 2021).

Jennifer Hetcht, *Doubt: A History*, (San Fransisco: HarperOne, 2004).

Bobby Conway, *Doubting Toward Faith: The Journey to Confident Christianity*, (Eugene, OR: Harvest House Publishers, 2015).

For engaging conversations about a whole range of belief-systems and philosophical questions, the BBC Radio 4 series *Beyond Belief* has much to recommend it. You can find past episodes of this on the BBC's website, or via an online search.

For introductions to a range of ideas about the Christian faith, the SPCK series *Little Books of Guidance* are good places to start.

For further reading on Christian history, doctrine and the Bible, the Oxford series *Very Short Introductions* provide a lot of material.

Printed in Great Britain
by Amazon